Yesterday's Blue

A Story About Childhood Depression

Cynthia Kaufman-Rose & Daniel-James F. Clarke
Illustrated by Cynthia Kaufman-Rose

Yesterday's Blue
A Story About Childhood Depression

Printed in the United States of America
Sunny Day Publishing, LLC
ISBN 978-0-9978006-6-1
Library of Congress Control Number: 2017908107

SUNNY DAY®
PUBLISHING, LLC

For my parents, Inge and Jozsi.

For Emma, Charlie-Asher and Clara, "…do justice, love mercy, and walk humbly…" Micah 6:8.

And for Kyle, constant and true.

—Cynthia

For all the children and adults who identify with this story: find help, and don't go it alone.

— Daniel

Something just
doesn't feel right.
Yesterday,
I couldn't sleep at
all. Today, all
I want to do is
sleep. I wish
I didn't have to
wake up.

Yesterday, I ate too
much. Today, my
stomach feels like
it's all knotted up.
I'm not hungry.
I just can't eat.

Other kids pay
attention at school.
I can't concentrate.
Other kids get excited
about everything.
I'm not interested
in anything.

Other kids laugh and have fun. Laughing doesn't seem fun to me. I feel angry with everyone. It's always my fault when things go wrong. I can't do anything right.

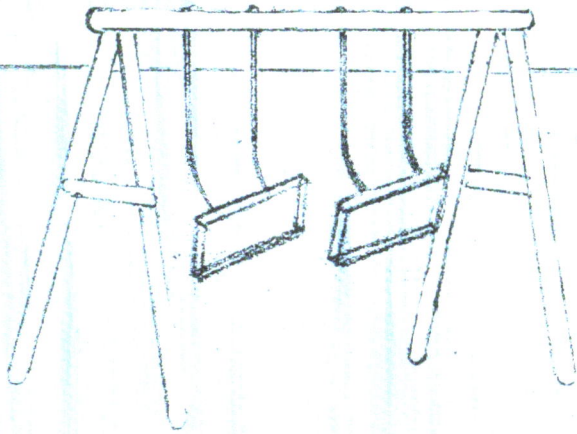

Some things I remember
make me really angry
and sad. Kids ask what's
wrong with me. Sometimes
I break and throw things,
but I don't know why.

My angry thoughts
and sad memories
won't go away.
I worry a lot.
I don't think anybody
likes me, so I spend
most of my time alone.

I used to be happy,
but now everything's
gloomy and blue.
Maybe something is
wrong with me.
I should talk to my
teacher. She likes me.

So I tell my teacher how
I feel. She says maybe
something is wrong,
and a doctor might be
able to help.

I talk to the doctor about everything. She says sometimes anger and sadness feel too deep, last for too long, and seem as if they will never end. This is a mood disorder called depression.

I learn that when difficult
or bad things happen
to me, it may cause
depression. Some kids
are just born with it. And
it doesn't always heal
completely. But it may get
better by talking about
thoughts and feelings,
starting some positive new
habits, and maybe taking
medicine.

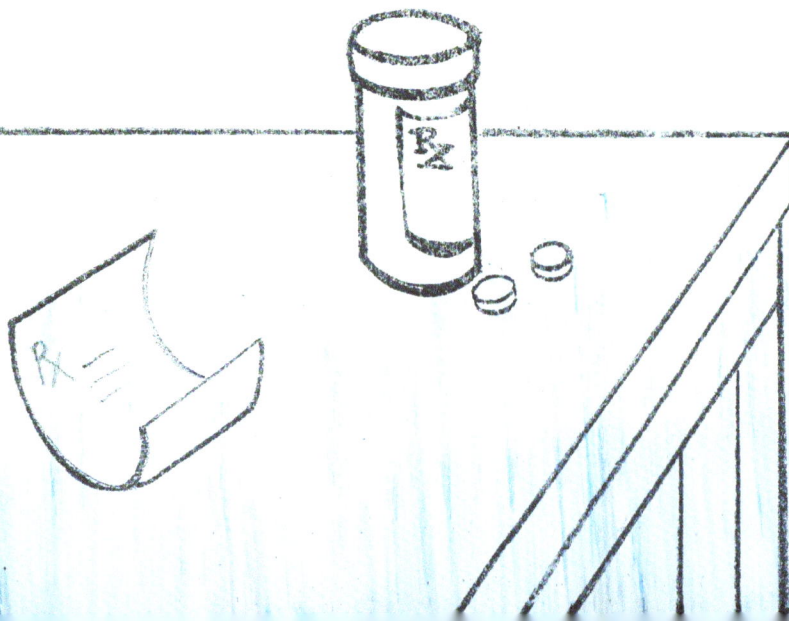

So I talk to the doctor often. I start replacing negative thoughts with positive thoughts. Instead of thinking it's always my fault when things go wrong, I think of how many things I can do right.

Instead of keeping my
feelings all knotted up
inside, I write them
down in a journal.
I write a long list of
angry and sad thoughts
and rip those pages out.
I write a longer list of
things I'm grateful for
and keep those pages
in. I write an even
longer list of things
I like about me.

Instead of dwelling on
sad thoughts and memories,
I accept them as part
of yesterday. Instead of
repeating old habits, I start
a new project today. Instead
of worrying, I make goals
for tomorrow.

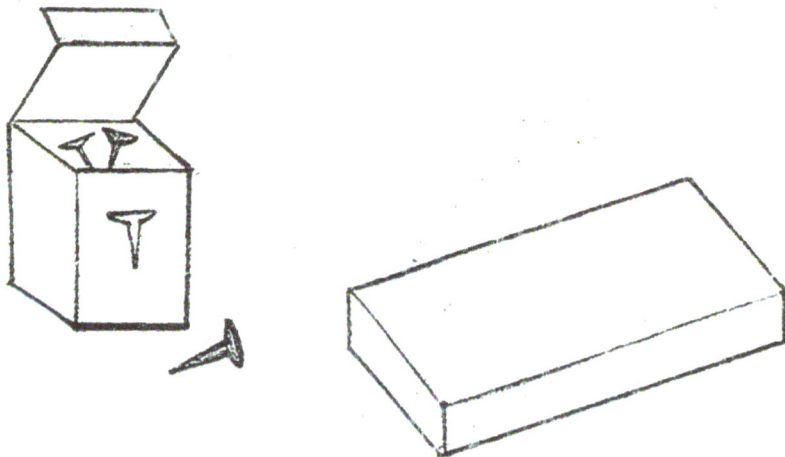

Instead of staying angry,
I do something kind for
someone else.

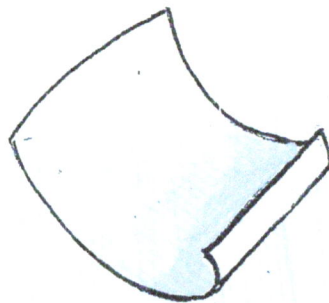

Instead of being alone,
I talk to someone who
needs a friend.

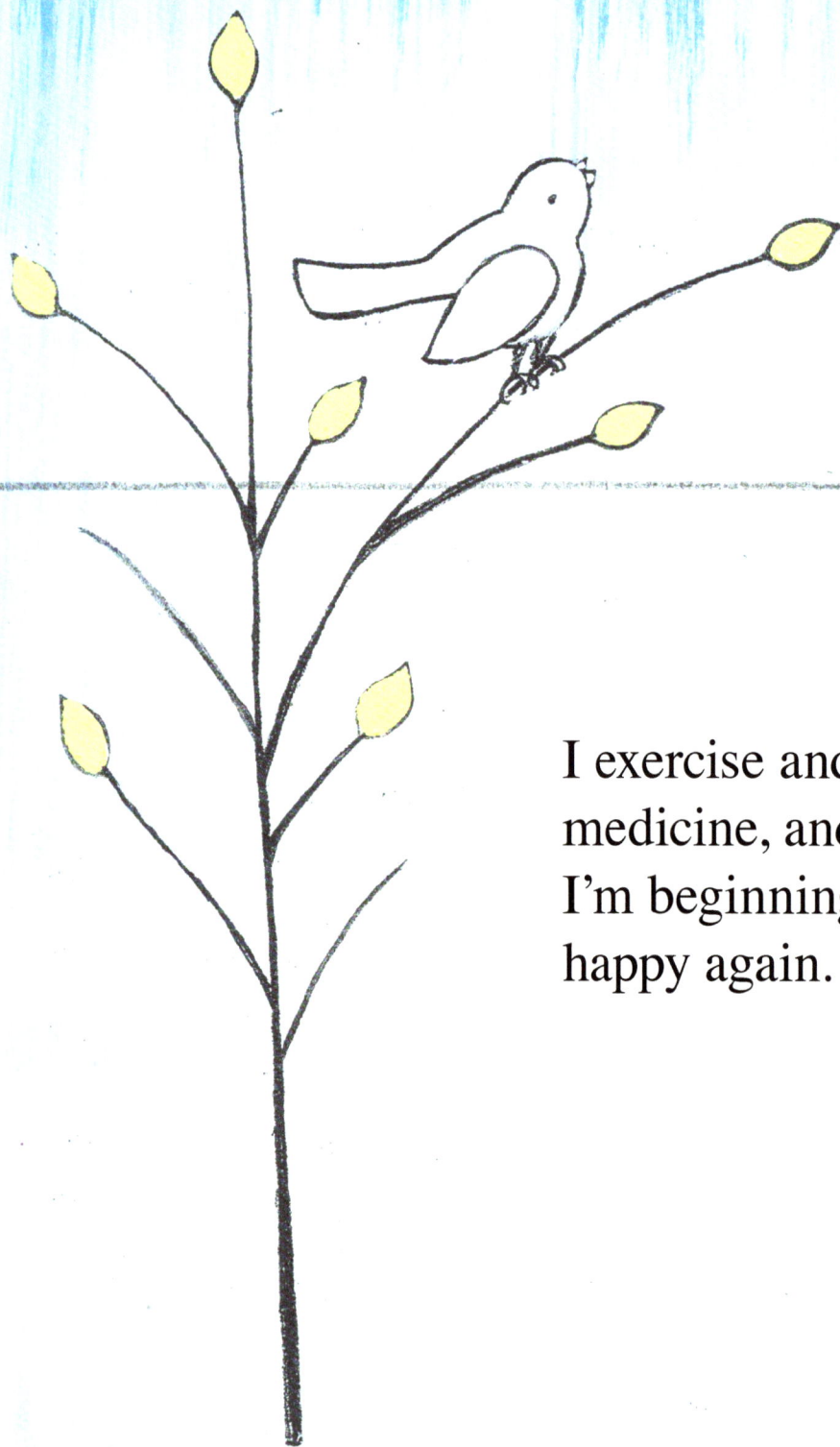

I exercise and take
medicine, and realize
I'm beginning to feel
happy again.

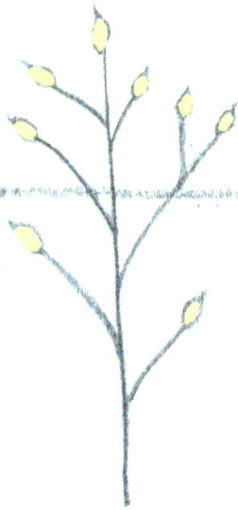

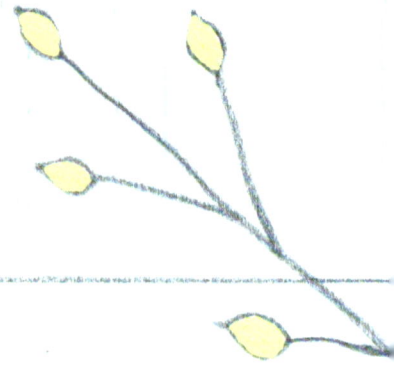

The depression doesn't
go away completely,
but I'm getting better
every day. I'm leaving
yesterday's blue
memories in the past.
I'm focusing on positive
thoughts today.
I'm hopeful for
tomorrow.

And I'm grateful to be me.

For parents, caregivers, and teachers:

Everyone feels irritable or down from time to time. But if sadness, anger, or hopelessness lasts for too long, depression may be the cause. Childhood depression is sadness that is persistent or feels unending. It is a serious mental health disorder that interferes with daily activities, relationships, and overall physical health.

Symptoms of childhood depression include:

Persistent feelings of sadness or hopelessness
Significant changes in appetite
Sleeplessness or excessive sleep
Chronic fatigue or lack of energy
Frequent complaints of physical ailments, stomachaches, or headaches
Anger or irritability
Struggles with concentration or thinking
Social withdrawal
Difficulties with daily routines, activities, and relationships
Feeling guilty or worthless
Excessive crying
Self-harming thoughts or behaviors

When these symptoms occur in your child frequently or daily for an extended period of time, they could be signs of depression. Fortunately, depression is a very treatable condition. Most children with depression respond well to therapy and medication. Talk to your child about feelings and things happening at home or school that may be troubling. Depending upon your child's needs, there are many resources, services, support groups, mental health professionals, and organizations available to help families and children affected by depression.

About the Authors:

Cynthia Kaufman-Rose, MFA, is a professional artist who was awarded several Ohio Arts Council individual artist fellowships. She was an Ohio Arts Council artist in residence for the Arts in Education program, and taught art in several colleges. Her interest in children's mental health opened a door to transform her imagery and words into children's books advocating for early intervention, mindfulness, and insight. She is co-author (with Daniel) of the children's book, *Daylight: A True Story of Childhood Schizophrenia*. Cynthia is married to Kyle and they have three children, Emma, Charlie-Asher, and Clara.

Daniel-James F. Clarke has an MA in counseling psychology, and has been an adjunct math professor at a state college. He is a US Army veteran, and has a son, Ryan-Christopher, who also served in the US Army. He raised his son as a single father while battling schizoaffective disorder, anxiety disorder, and PTSD. Having gone through depression during childhood, he takes a special interest in sharing his experiences to help other children. Daniel is co-author (with Cynthia) of the children's book, *Daylight: A True Story of Childhood Schizophrenia*, and author of a book for adults titled *Fragments: My Journey with Schizophrenia*.

* 9 7 8 0 9 9 7 8 0 0 6 6 1 *